The Inner Naturalist Journal

Winter & Early Spring
JANUARY – MARCH

REST & AWAKENING

developed by **Lari Jo Wallace Edwards**

Copyright © 2025 Lari Jo Wallace Edwards

ISBN: 979-8-9990023-3-4

All rights reserved. No part of this book may be reproduced or transmitted in any form or by any means, electronic or mechanical, including photocopying, recording or by any information storage and retrieval system without written permission of the publisher, except for the inclusion of brief quotations in a review.

INTRODUCTION

I'm so glad you're here. I believe these practices—or perhaps they believe in us—find their way into our lives when we're ready to soften, to rest, to listen to what's stirring quietly beneath the surface.

This journal—covering January through March—is for the part of you that longs to rest deeply and begin again, slowly and intentionally.

For many years, I pushed through winter as if it were an inconvenience—something to endure until brighter days returned. But Nature has shown me otherwise. Beneath the stillness, the earth is alive with quiet preparation. Seeds are gathering strength underground. Trees hold their breath before the bloom. Even the coldest days are part of the sacred rhythm of renewal.

Winter and Early Spring remind us that healing and growth often happen in the unseen places. This is a season to pause, to breathe, and to trust the timing of your own becoming. This is a time for rest and reflection. A time for planting seeds of intention. A time to listen for what is ready to awaken within you.

Inside this journal, you'll find:

- Reflection prompts for slowing down and reconnecting with your inner wisdom
- Nature-based rituals for rest, release, and renewal
- Seasonal practices to gently awaken your body and spirit
- Guided questions to help you plant seeds for what's next

You'll be invited to sit quietly and notice the hush of winter's breath. To watch the light return—minute by minute—as each day grows longer. To feel the courage that comes with small beginnings. To plant a seed, in soil or in spirit, for something new you wish to nurture. Through journaling, sketching, mindful wandering, and simple moments of noticing, you'll discover that you, too, are part of nature's great unfolding—never static, always cycling, always becoming.

This season reminds us:

- Rest is not a pause in life — it's part of the life cycle itself.
- Stillness is not absence — it's where clarity is born.
- New beginnings don't require force — only faith.

Let this journal be your hearth in the cold months—a place to curl inward, reflect deeply, and gently awaken to what's next. You're not behind. You're right on time. And as always, I'll be walking this path with you—step by step, breath by breath, bud by bud.

Happy Nature Connecting!

—Lari Jo

The Wheel of the Year

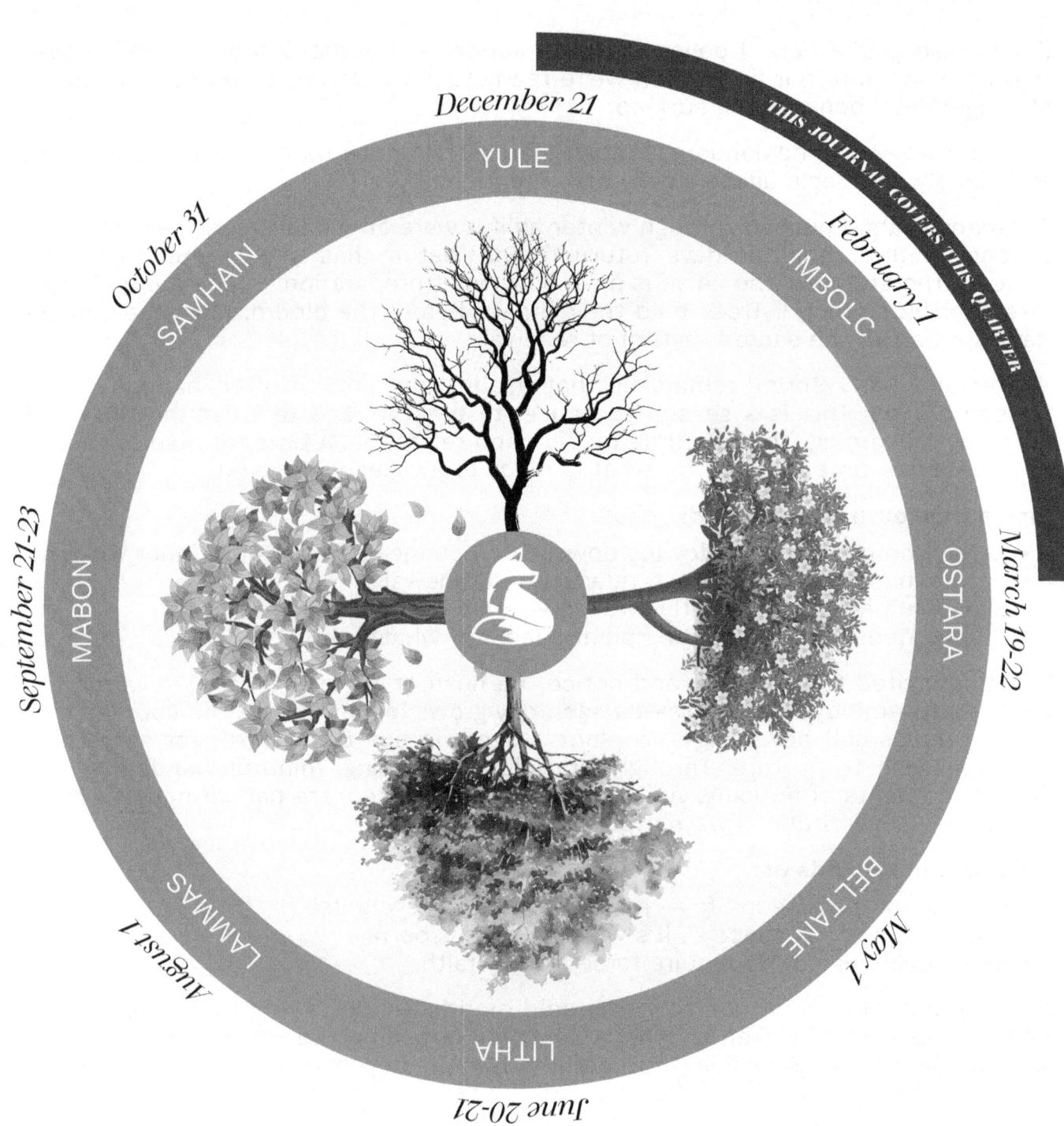

The Wheel of the Year

Living these cycles helps you to love and respect nature, and live in harmony with the earth. One of the main beliefs is "Harm None." This includes animals, humans, and nature.

① SAMAHAIN
Moving Towards Winter

Samhain is the celebration that is the origin the final harvest. It is a time of deep work. Slow down and honor the past and any Death that has occurred while embracing the dark season of the year. Take time to reflect on the past year and set intentions for the upcoming year that starts with Yule.

② YULE
Winter Solstice

Yule celebrates rebirth and renewal. This is because the shortest day and longest night occur on the solstice. After the solstice, the days start to get longer, and Yule celebrates the beginning of the return of the sun. With shorter days, we may need more rest and experience less energy. For many of us, our inclination is to withdraw indoors in Winter, but you can still (and should) enjoy nature in the winter. Celebrate with story telling, Set goals for they new longer productive days ahead, feast with family and friends, Spend time giving back to nature.

③ IMBOLC
Moving Towards Spring

The celebration of Imbolc is a celebration of fire and light. It symbolizes the halfway point between the winter solstice (Yule) and the spring equinox (Ostara). The word "imbolc" means "in the belly of the Mother," because the seeds of spring are beginning to stir in the belly of Mother Earth. Around this time of year, many herd animals give birth to their first offspring of the year, or are heavily pregnant. This creation of life's milk is a part of the symbolic hope for spring. This is a time when shoots begin to sprout, buds begin to peon and light and warmth are beginning to touch our days. Celebrate with Inspiration and time in nature, set your wellness goals, and plant seeds literally and figuratively.

④ OSTARA
Spring Equinox

Ostara represents spring and new beginnings. Ostara symbolizes fertility, rebirth, and renewal. This time of year marked the beginning of the agricultural cycle, and farmers would start planting seeds. Ostara is a day of perfect balance when the sun can be seen directly above the earth's equator. It is the time when light and dark are completely equal. One might go outside to meditate and perform a simple ritual to welcome the spring, go outside, color eggs, tend to your spring garden, and feast with family.

⑤ BELTANE
Moving Towards Summer

Beltane falls about halfway between the spring equinox (Ostara) and the coming summer solstice, (Litha). The holiday celebrates spring as its peak, and the coming summer. his holiday is associated very strongly with fertility, lust, power and abundance. Decorate with fresh flowers, take action on projects, enjoy abundance, love, and passion. This is a time of dancing, fairies, and fun! Enjoy it!

⑥ LITHA
Summer Solstice

Litha occurs on the summer solstice, and celebrates the beginning of summer. It celebrates the sun's power and the longest day of the year. Celebrate by connecting with nature on a deeper level; walks in a forest or natural location, walking barefoot (grounding) either in your backyard or on a beach can help you feel connected to the earth as can sitting by a bonfire, meditating outside, or just gardening.

⑦ LAMMAS
Autumn

Lammas, which is about halfway between the summer solstice (Litha) and the fall equinox (Mabon). It celebrates the first harvest or grain harvest. Celebrate by baking bread, giving thanks, reflect on everything you have created this year, make a cornhusk doll or collect seeds for the next year.

⑧ MABON
Autumn Equinox

Mabon celebrates the autumnal equinox. It celebrates the second harvest which includes berries. It is a time of balance the days and nights are once again equal. As the harvest completes, the leaves begin to change color and the warmth of summer is replaced by pleasant, breezy days. This is a time to reap the bounty of summer, to plant new seeds for the spring, to contemplate new ideas, and to make medicine. Celebrate with introspection and grace, set intentions that involve decrease and reduction such as ending bad relationships, unhealthy habits or self destructive beliefs, write down your blessings from the past year, have a picnic in nature and decorate your porch for fall.

The Wheel of the Year
Intention Setting

IMBOLC
Moving Towards Spring

How will I connect to nature this season?

What actions will I take?

How will I enjoy abundance? Love? Passion?

OSTARA
Spring Equinox

How will I connect to nature this season?

What actions will I take?

How will I enjoy abundance? Love? Passion?

Vision Board

HEALTH	FAMILY	RELATIONSHIPS
FINANCE	CAREER	PERSONAL DEVELOPMENT
LOVE	SKILLS	SPIRITUALITY
FUN & RECREATION	KNOWLEDGE	SOCIAL

90-Day Overview

January

SUN	MON	TUE	WED	THU	FRI	SAT
○	○	○	○	○	○	○
○	○	○	○	○	○	○
○	○	○	○	○	○	○
○	○	○	○	○	○	○
○	○	○	○	○	○	○

February

SUN	MON	TUE	WED	THU	FRI	SAT
○	○	○	○	○	○	○
○	○	○	○	○	○	○
○	○	○	○	○	○	○
○	○	○	○	○	○	○
○	○	○	○	○	○	○

March

SUN	MON	TUE	WED	THU	FRI	SAT
○	○	○	○	○	○	○
○	○	○	○	○	○	○
○	○	○	○	○	○	○
○	○	○	○	○	○	○
○	○	○	○	○	○	○

Winter & Early Spring Season Goals

Align your personal growth with nature's rhythms.

MESSAGE TO MYSELF THIS SEASON

THIS SEASON'S TOP 3 GOALS

1.

2.

3.

TO DO THIS SEASON

☐
☐
☐
☐
☐
☐
☐
☐
☐
☐

PEOPLE I NEED TO REACH OUT TO

♥
♥
♥
♥
♥

Winter
Season Mindset

One thing in nature that inspires or excites me this season is...

A positive phrase I can repeat to myself while grounded in nature is...

Someone who needs my full presence and energy this season is...

A situation that might stress me out or trip me up this season could be...

> *... and I will take a moment in nature to breathe, observe, or connect before responding as my best self.*

Someone I could surprise with a nature-inspired note, gift, or moment of appreciation is...

One action I could take this season to embody excellence or bring joy to my environment is...

One bold step I could take this season that mirrors nature's courage and resilience is...

If I were a guide walking alongside myself in nature, I would encourage myself with this...

The big picture I have to keep in mind this season is that I am growing, like the cycles of nature, steadily towards...

> *I would end this season feeling proud if I make sure to spend time appreciating the small, beautiful details in my life, just like noticing a flower or sunset.*

Journal

Sit Spot

A sit spot is simply a favorite place in your nearby nature that you visit regularly to cultivate awareness as you expand your senses.

By choosing one place outside that you visit over and over again, it teaches you to develop the most ancient parts of human awareness and gradually acquire enhanced sensitivity to nature.

Richard Louv talks about this by saying that nature is like *vitamins for the human mind*.

It's a way of giving yourself the mental, emotional, spiritual, and creative fuel for your own personal evolution in modern times.

People who practice Sit Spot enjoy:

- Improved sensory awareness and sensory acuity
- Enhanced critical thinking, problem solving, deductive and inductive thinking (especially when Sit Spot is associated with studies in animal tracking)
- Improved creativity
- Better naturalist skills, wildlife tracking, bird language, plant identification, etc.
- Greater capacity for releasing emotions and negative thinking through a natural state of meditation that promotes mental and physical relaxation
- Close encounters with birds, plants, trees and animals that inspire a sense of awe and wonder
- A renewed sense of happiness and joy coming from inside
- A developing sense of inner vitality and razor sharp focus
- Greater peace & joy in daily life
- A sense of connection to the past ancestry of our species and planet
- Greater flexibility of consciousness, enabling you to see life from a wider and more balanced perspective.

Humans are biologically designed to fall in love with nature, and we operate at our highest capacity when we get to live out our biological potential! Now that we've talked about why sit spot matters... let's take a closer look at how you can actually do all this!

KEEP IT SIMPLE!

One of the biggest secrets to success with having a sit spot in nature is to keep your practice routines extremely simple. Don't go far from home and visit it often. At least 3 times a week.

Remember – a sit spot is really about giving yourself the opportunity to quiet your mind and focus your senses on nature (rather than technology or any other distractions).

And this is something that can be done almost anywhere, anytime. Even 5 minutes sitting in some grass with nearby ground feeding birds is all you really need to get started and be successful. I suggest working toward at least 20 minutes each time you visit your sit spot.

In it's most basic form:

1. You just go outside.
2. Find a place in nature to sit down.
3. Practice opening your senses and observing nature.
4. If an intention is set, open your heart and see what nature has to teach you
5. Repeat as often as you can.

You will set an intention and see what nature has to teach you that day. Enjoy your time and notice how your feelings of calm seem to grow with each time you visit your sit spot!

December

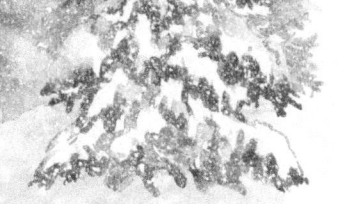

YEAR: _____

SUN	MON	TUE	WED	THU	FRI	SAT
○	○	○	○	○	○	○
○	○	○	○	○	○	○
○	○	○	○	○	○	○
○	○	○	○	○	○	○
○	○	○	○	○	○	○

December

PRIORITIES	
1.	
2.	
3.	

WEEK: _____

through _____

MONDAY
- [ ] _____
- [ ] _____
- [ ] _____
- [ ] _____
- [ ] _____
- [ ] _____

Sit directly on the ground — grass, dirt, snow, or floor. Feel the solid support beneath you. Imagine the heartbeat of the Earth steady and strong. Journal your reflections: *What grounding practices help me feel safe and connected? What do I hear when I truly listen to the Earth?*

TUESDAY
- [ ] _____
- [ ] _____
- [ ] _____
- [ ] _____
- [ ] _____
- [ ] _____

FRIDAY
- [ ] _____
- [ ] _____
- [ ] _____
- [ ] _____
- [ ] _____
- [ ] _____

WEDNESDAY
- [ ] _____
- [ ] _____
- [ ] _____
- [ ] _____
- [ ] _____
- [ ] _____

SATURDAY
- [ ] _____
- [ ] _____
- [ ] _____
- [ ] _____
- [ ] _____
- [ ] _____

THURSDAY
- [ ] _____
- [ ] _____
- [ ] _____
- [ ] _____
- [ ] _____
- [ ] _____

SUNDAY
- [ ] _____
- [ ] _____
- [ ] _____
- [ ] _____
- [ ] _____
- [ ] _____

Color in one snowflake for each block of 17 minutes that you connect with nature per week (sit spots, mindful walks, outdoor rituals). *Aim to spend 17 minutes a day in nature.*

WEEKLY GRATITUDE

_____
_____
_____
_____
_____
_____
_____
_____

MIND: *What clarity has come to me, and how can I honor it?*

BODY: *How do I feel when I let myself fully bask in the season's warmth and abundance?*

SPIRIT: *What does it mean to shine fully, and where do I hold back?*

WEEKLY NATURE SKETCH

WEEKLY TO-DO

○ _____
○ _____
○ _____
○ _____
○ _____
○ _____
○ _____
○ _____
○ _____
○ _____
○ _____
○ _____
○ _____
○ _____
○ _____
○ _____
○ _____
○ _____

MEAL PLAN

B: _____
L: _____
D: _____

B: _____
L: _____
D: _____

B: _____
L: _____
D: _____

B: _____
L: _____
D: _____

B: _____
L: _____
D: _____

B: _____
L: _____
D: _____

B: _____
L: _____
D: _____

Journal

Your Personal Wheel of Well-Being

Welcome!

This Personal Wheel is a snapshot of your life today — a map showing where you're thriving and where a little more sunlight, water, and nurturing might help you grow. Just like a tree needs sunlight, soil, and water to flourish, we too need intentional care across different areas of life.

Before You Start:

Remember that research shows spending just 17 minutes a day in nature begins to create real change in your brain, body, and spirit. As you fill out this wheel, I invite you to imagine yourself like a strong, beautiful oak tree — standing firm, growing, and reaching for the sun.

Here's how to fill it out:

1. Look at each section of your Wheel.

Each area has two parts (Personal and Business, where applicable). You'll be scoring yourself from 1 to 10:
- 1 means you feel depleted or lacking in that area — like a dry riverbed.
- 10 means you are absolutely thriving — like a lush forest after a spring rain.

2. Sections to score:

- ***Spiritual Connection***
    - Personal: How connected do you feel to your own sense of spirit, inner peace, or purpose?
    - Community: How connected do you feel spiritually with others, through community, group practices, or shared values?
- ***Emotional Stress Level***
    - Business: How often do you feel calm and resilient versus overwhelmed in your work life?
    - Personal: How well do you handle emotional ups and downs in your personal life?
- ***Physical Health***
    - Exercise: How consistent and satisfying is your movement practice?
    - Nutrition: How nourished and energized do you feel by what you eat?
- ***Financial Health***
    - Personal: How secure and in control do you feel about your personal finances?
    - Business: How stable and sustainable is your business or work income?

- ***Curiosity***
    - Personal: How often are you exploring, learning, or trying new things just for yourself?
    - Business: How often are you staying curious, growing, and innovating in your work or business life?

3. Be honest and gentle.

Nature doesn't rush her seasons, and neither should you. Today's score isn't about judgment — it's about awareness. Even a tiny acorn eventually becomes a mighty oak.

4. After scoring:

- Notice the areas that feel strong — celebrate them!
- Notice the areas that feel tender — these are invitations for gentle attention.
- Remember: Just 17 minutes a day in nature can begin to shift your energy in any of these areas. Even a walk under the trees, sitting by a garden, or feeling the breeze on your face counts.

5. Plant a Seed of Intention.

Choose one small, nurturing action to tend to the areas that feel tender as you move into the new season. Examples:
- If your Personal Spiritual Connection feels low, you might commit to sitting under a tree for five minutes each morning.
- If your Business Emotional Stress Level is high, you might block out one afternoon a week to work outside or take mindful breaks.
- If your Physical Exercise score is low, you could begin with a 10-minute nature walk after dinner each evening.
- If your Personal Finances feel strained, you could start a gratitude journal focused on non-material abundance found in nature.
- If your Curiosity in Business feels dull, you might visit a botanical garden or attend an outdoor workshop to spark new ideas.

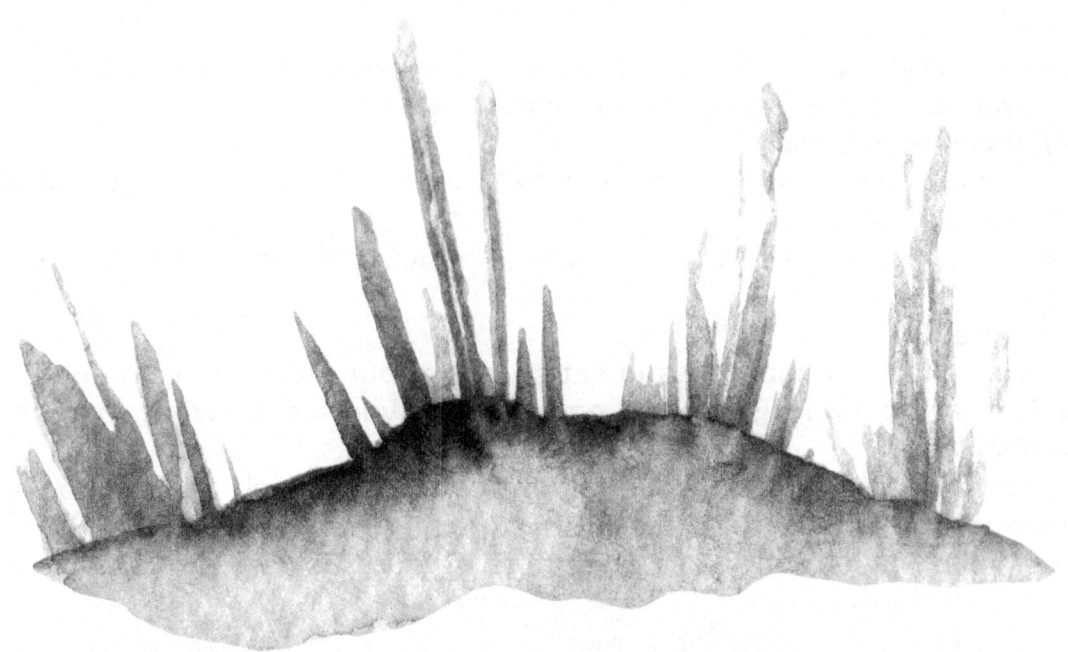

January Wheel of Wellbeing

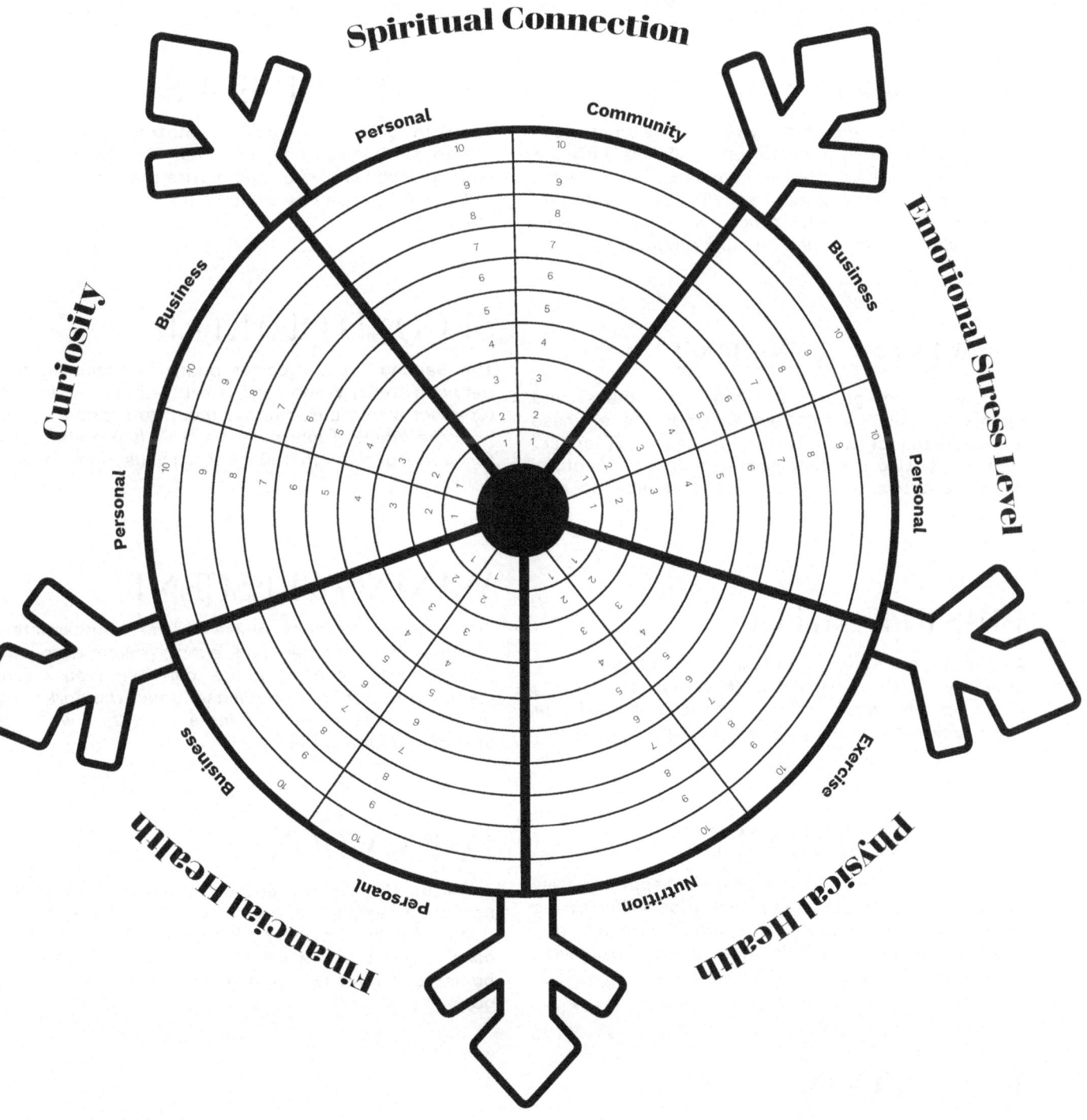

Seeds of Intention: _____
_____
_____
_____

The Phases of the Moon

NEW MOON

The New Moon is the first day of the new lunar cycle. In may perspectives, this phase is linked with the Dark Moon, consider your intentions, sow seeds, tend to the shadow dream, scheme, plot, and plan, *(This is an excellent time for shadow work, connecting with spirit, and spiritual practicing.)*

WAXING CRESCENT

As the moon grows, so can your plans and intentions. The Waxing Crescent moon is a phase approximately between two to six days old. *(Connect with the Waxing Crescent phase to build momentum, bring an action to your dreams, and begin a new process.)*

FIRST QUARTER

A First Quarter Moon is approximately between six to nine days in the lunar cycle. *(Much like the Waxing Crescent, this phase can help you work toward your goals, develop habits, and move, through processes.)*

WAXING GIBBOUS

The Waxing Gibbous moon phase is approximately between Six to thirteen days old. *(Connect with the Waxing Gibbous phase for spiritual practice and intention setting towards abundance, expansion, growth, and working toward culmination.)*

FULL MOON

The Full Moon phase is approximately between thirteen and fifteen days old. *(The Full Moon is a celebration of wholeness, release, fulfillment, sensuality, and abundance spiritual practice.)*

WANING GIBBOUS

The Waning Gibbous moon is approximately between fifteen and twenty-one days old. *(Connect with the Waning Gibbous phase to integrate the lessons of the full moon, deepen understanding, and continue to release.)*

SECOND QUARTER

The Second (Last) Quarter phase is approximately between twenty-one and twenty-three days old. *(Connect with a Last Quarter moon to support rituals with the intent of internal work. This is a great moon for working through the subconscious and shadow work.)*

WANING CRESCENT

The Waning Crescent phase is the approximately between twenty-three and twenty-seven days old. *(The Waning Crescent phase can help you clean, clear, purify, banish, and release. Under the darkening moon, connect more and more with that which is liminal and intuitive for you.)*

DARK MOON

The Dark Moon is the end of the lunar cycle before beginning again, taking place at approximately twenty-seven to twenty-nine days. *(The Dark Moon asks you to turn inward, to reflect and rest, and to banish and release anything that you're ready to let go of.)*

The Phases of the Moon
January Intention Setting

WAXING MOON
Taking Action, Building Momentum

What inspired action can I take now to move closer to my intentions?

DATE: _____

FULL MOON
Releasing, Celebrating, Acknowledging

What am I ready to celebrate, release, and honor from this cycle to make space for what's next?

DATE: _____

WANING MOON
Releasing, Letting Go

What thoughts, habits, or patterns am I ready to let go of to align more fully with my purpose?

DATE: _____

NEW MOON
Planting Seeds, Setting Goals

What intention or desire do I want to plant and nurture in the cycle ahead?

DATE: _____

January

YEAR: _____

SUN	MON	TUE	WED
○	○	○	○
○	○	○	○
○	○	○	○
○	○	○	○
○	○	○	○

WINTER WALK OF AWARENESS

Take a slow, mindful walk outdoors and let the winter world guide your senses. Notice how nature rests — the bare branches, frozen ground, muted colors, and quiet air. Even in stillness, there is life. Let the landscape mirror your own rhythm of rest and reflection. What does rest look like in your life right now?

THU	FRI	SAT

JOURNAL PROMPT

What wisdom can I hear only in the quiet?

January

PRIORITIES
1.
2.
3.

WEEK: _____
through _____

MONDAY
- [ ] _____
- [ ] _____
- [ ] _____
- [ ] _____
- [ ] _____
- [ ] _____

As the new year dawns, the world is still and hushed. Step outside and breathe in the cold morning air. Notice the way the frost clings to grass or branches — quiet yet resilient. Let this stillness invite you to begin slowly. Journal your reflections: *How can I honor rest as I enter this new year? What does beginning gently look like for me?*

TUESDAY
- [ ] _____
- [ ] _____
- [ ] _____
- [ ] _____
- [ ] _____
- [ ] _____

FRIDAY
- [ ] _____
- [ ] _____
- [ ] _____
- [ ] _____
- [ ] _____
- [ ] _____

WEDNESDAY
- [ ] _____
- [ ] _____
- [ ] _____
- [ ] _____
- [ ] _____
- [ ] _____

SATURDAY
- [ ] _____
- [ ] _____
- [ ] _____
- [ ] _____
- [ ] _____
- [ ] _____

THURSDAY
- [ ] _____
- [ ] _____
- [ ] _____
- [ ] _____
- [ ] _____
- [ ] _____

SUNDAY
- [ ] _____
- [ ] _____
- [ ] _____
- [ ] _____
- [ ] _____
- [ ] _____

Color in one snowflake for each block of 17 minutes that you connect with nature per week (sit spots, mindful walks, outdoor rituals). *Aim to spend 17 minutes a day in nature.*

WEEKLY GRATITUDE

WEEKLY NATURE SKETCH

MIND: *What clarity has come to me, and how can I honor it?*

BODY: *How do I feel when I let myself fully bask in the season's warmth and abundance?*

SPIRIT: *What does it mean to shine fully, and where do I hold back?*

WEEKLY TO-DO

MEAL PLAN

B:
L:
D:

B:
L:
D:

B:
L:
D:

B:
L:
D:

B:
L:
D:

B:
L:
D:

B:
L:
D:

January

PRIORITIES
1.
2.
3.

WEEK: _____
through _____

MONDAY
- [ ] _____
- [ ] _____
- [ ] _____
- [ ] _____
- [ ] _____
- [ ] _____

Take a slow walk in nature. Notice the quiet rhythm beneath the surface — the roots, the soil, the life unseen. Winter reminds us that growth doesn't always look like movement. Journal your reflections: *Where am I growing quietly, even if no one can see it? What inner work is happening beneath the surface?*

TUESDAY
- [ ] _____
- [ ] _____
- [ ] _____
- [ ] _____
- [ ] _____
- [ ] _____

FRIDAY
- [ ] _____
- [ ] _____
- [ ] _____
- [ ] _____
- [ ] _____
- [ ] _____

WEDNESDAY
- [ ] _____
- [ ] _____
- [ ] _____
- [ ] _____
- [ ] _____
- [ ] _____

SATURDAY
- [ ] _____
- [ ] _____
- [ ] _____
- [ ] _____
- [ ] _____
- [ ] _____

THURSDAY
- [ ] _____
- [ ] _____
- [ ] _____
- [ ] _____
- [ ] _____
- [ ] _____

SUNDAY
- [ ] _____
- [ ] _____
- [ ] _____
- [ ] _____
- [ ] _____
- [ ] _____

Color in one snowflake for each block of 17 minutes that you connect with nature per week (sit spots, mindful walks, outdoor rituals). *Aim to spend 17 minutes a day in nature.*

WEEKLY GRATITUDE

_____
_____
_____
_____
_____
_____
_____
_____
_____

MIND: *What clarity has come to me, and how can I honor it?*

BODY: *How do I feel when I let myself fully bask in the season's warmth and abundance?*

SPIRIT: *What does it mean to shine fully, and where do I hold back?*

WEEKLY NATURE SKETCH

WEEKLY TO-DO

○ _____
○ _____
○ _____
○ _____
○ _____
○ _____
○ _____
○ _____
○ _____
○ _____
○ _____
○ _____
○ _____
○ _____
○ _____
○ _____
○ _____
○ _____

MEAL PLAN

B: _____
L: _____
D: _____

B: _____
L: _____
D: _____

B: _____
L: _____
D: _____

B: _____
L: _____
D: _____

B: _____
L: _____
D: _____

B: _____
L: _____
D: _____

B: _____
L: _____
D: _____

January

PRIORITIES
1.
2.
3.

WEEK: _____

through _____

MONDAY
- ☐ _____
- ☐ _____
- ☐ _____
- ☐ _____
- ☐ _____
- ☐ _____

Find a tree that has lost its leaves. Place your hand on its bark and feel its strength even in dormancy. Trees teach us that we can be both bare and alive. Journal your reflections: *Where in my life do I feel stripped back? How can I trust the strength in my own stillness?*

TUESDAY
- ☐ _____
- ☐ _____
- ☐ _____
- ☐ _____
- ☐ _____
- ☐ _____

FRIDAY
- ☐ _____
- ☐ _____
- ☐ _____
- ☐ _____
- ☐ _____
- ☐ _____

WEDNESDAY
- ☐ _____
- ☐ _____
- ☐ _____
- ☐ _____
- ☐ _____
- ☐ _____

SATURDAY
- ☐ _____
- ☐ _____
- ☐ _____
- ☐ _____
- ☐ _____
- ☐ _____

THURSDAY
- ☐ _____
- ☐ _____
- ☐ _____
- ☐ _____
- ☐ _____
- ☐ _____

SUNDAY
- ☐ _____
- ☐ _____
- ☐ _____
- ☐ _____
- ☐ _____
- ☐ _____

Color in one snowflake for each block of 17 minutes that you connect with nature per week (sit spots, mindful walks, outdoor rituals). *Aim to spend 17 minutes a day in nature.*

WEEKLY GRATITUDE

_____
_____
_____
_____
_____
_____
_____
_____
_____
_____

MIND: *What clarity has come to me, and how can I honor it?*

BODY: *How do I feel when I let myself fully bask in the season's warmth and abundance?*

SPIRIT: *What does it mean to shine fully, and where do I hold back?*

WEEKLY NATURE SKETCH

WEEKLY TO-DO

- ☐ _____
- ☐ _____
- ☐ _____
- ☐ _____
- ☐ _____
- ☐ _____
- ☐ _____
- ☐ _____
- ☐ _____
- ☐ _____
- ☐ _____
- ☐ _____
- ☐ _____
- ☐ _____
- ☐ _____
- ☐ _____
- ☐ _____
- ☐ _____

MEAL PLAN

B: _____
L: _____
D: _____

B: _____
L: _____
D: _____

B: _____
L: _____
D: _____

B: _____
L: _____
D: _____

B: _____
L: _____
D: _____

B: _____
L: _____
D: _____

B: _____
L: _____
D: _____

January

	PRIORITIES
	1.
	2.
	3.

WEEK: _____

through _____

MONDAY
- [ ] _____
- [ ] _____
- [ ] _____
- [ ] _____
- [ ] _____
- [ ] _____

Watch the evening sky as the sun sets early. Let the gathering darkness remind you of your own need for rest. Light a candle and sit quietly for a few moments, feeling the warmth against the chill. Journal your reflections: *What does the darkness offer me? What might I find when I stop resisting stillness?*

TUESDAY
- [ ] _____
- [ ] _____
- [ ] _____
- [ ] _____
- [ ] _____
- [ ] _____

FRIDAY
- [ ] _____
- [ ] _____
- [ ] _____
- [ ] _____
- [ ] _____
- [ ] _____

WEDNESDAY
- [ ] _____
- [ ] _____
- [ ] _____
- [ ] _____
- [ ] _____
- [ ] _____

SATURDAY
- [ ] _____
- [ ] _____
- [ ] _____
- [ ] _____
- [ ] _____
- [ ] _____

THURSDAY
- [ ] _____
- [ ] _____
- [ ] _____
- [ ] _____
- [ ] _____
- [ ] _____

SUNDAY
- [ ] _____
- [ ] _____
- [ ] _____
- [ ] _____
- [ ] _____
- [ ] _____

Color in one snowflake for each block of 17 minutes that you connect with nature per week (sit spots, mindful walks, outdoor rituals). *Aim to spend 17 minutes a day in nature.*

WEEKLY GRATITUDE

_____
_____
_____
_____
_____
_____
_____
_____

MIND: *What clarity has come to me, and how can I honor it?*

BODY: *How do I feel when I let myself fully bask in the season's warmth and abundance?*

SPIRIT: *What does it mean to shine fully, and where do I hold back?*

WEEKLY NATURE SKETCH

WEEKLY TO-DO

○ _____
○ _____
○ _____
○ _____
○ _____
○ _____
○ _____
○ _____
○ _____
○ _____
○ _____
○ _____
○ _____
○ _____
○ _____
○ _____
○ _____
○ _____

MEAL PLAN

B: _____
L: _____
D: _____

B: _____
L: _____
D: _____

B: _____
L: _____
D: _____

B: _____
L: _____
D: _____

B: _____
L: _____
D: _____

B: _____
L: _____
D: _____

B: _____
L: _____
D: _____

January

PRIORITIES
1.
2.
3.

WEEK: _____
through _____

MONDAY
- [ ] _____
- [ ] _____
- [ ] _____
- [ ] _____
- [ ] _____
- [ ] _____

As the month closes, look back at how winter has shaped you so far. Notice one way you've softened or slowed. Step outside and offer gratitude to the land around you — the soil that holds you, the air that sustains you. Journal your reflections: *What has winter taught me about myself? What can I thank this season for?*

TUESDAY
- [ ] _____
- [ ] _____
- [ ] _____
- [ ] _____
- [ ] _____
- [ ] _____

FRIDAY
- [ ] _____
- [ ] _____
- [ ] _____
- [ ] _____
- [ ] _____
- [ ] _____

WEDNESDAY
- [ ] _____
- [ ] _____
- [ ] _____
- [ ] _____
- [ ] _____
- [ ] _____

SATURDAY
- [ ] _____
- [ ] _____
- [ ] _____
- [ ] _____
- [ ] _____
- [ ] _____

THURSDAY
- [ ] _____
- [ ] _____
- [ ] _____
- [ ] _____
- [ ] _____
- [ ] _____

SUNDAY
- [ ] _____
- [ ] _____
- [ ] _____
- [ ] _____
- [ ] _____
- [ ] _____

Color in one snowflake for each block of 17 minutes that you connect with nature per week (sit spots, mindful walks, outdoor rituals). *Aim to spend 17 minutes a day in nature.*

WEEKLY GRATITUDE

_____
_____
_____
_____
_____
_____
_____
_____

MIND: *What clarity has come to me, and how can I honor it?*

BODY: *How do I feel when I let myself fully bask in the season's warmth and abundance?*

SPIRIT: *What does it mean to shine fully, and where do I hold back?*

WEEKLY NATURE SKETCH

WEEKLY TO-DO

- ☐ _____
- ☐ _____
- ☐ _____
- ☐ _____
- ☐ _____
- ☐ _____
- ☐ _____
- ☐ _____
- ☐ _____
- ☐ _____
- ☐ _____
- ☐ _____
- ☐ _____
- ☐ _____
- ☐ _____
- ☐ _____
- ☐ _____

MEAL PLAN

B: _____
L: _____
D: _____

B: _____
L: _____
D: _____

B: _____
L: _____
D: _____

B: _____
L: _____
D: _____

B: _____
L: _____
D: _____

B: _____
L: _____
D: _____

B: _____
L: _____
D: _____

January
Sit Spot
REFLECTIONS

What is nature teaching me?

How am I growing into my true self?

What steps am I taking toward my soul's passion?

January
Sit Spot
REFLECTIONS

Journal

Journal

Journal

Journal

IMBOLC

FEBRUARY 1
A Season of Awakening & Inner Light

Overview

Imbolc (pronounced Im-bolk or Im-olc) marks the midpoint between winter and spring—traditionally celebrated around February 1st or 2nd. It is a festival of light returning, hope rekindling, and the first whispers of new life stirring beneath the soil. The name itself means "in the belly," symbolizing both the womb of the Earth and the creative spark gestating within us. This is Brigid's time—the goddess of hearth, poetry, healing, and inspiration. Nature begins to awaken: snowdrops push through frost, lambs are born, and the days grow noticeably longer. Imbolc invites us to honor our inner flame and nurture the tender beginnings of dreams not yet in bloom.

Nature's Invitation (Sit Spot Practice)

Find a quiet spot outdoors where you can notice the subtle signs of renewal—perhaps a patch of emerging green or a bird's tentative song. Sit with the cool air and the soft returning light. What within you is ready to awaken after winter's stillness? Close your eyes and feel your heartbeat as a small flame in your chest. Feed it with breath and intention. Whisper gratitude for what is beginning, even if unseen.

Reflective Focus:

- What creative spark or vision is stirring within me?
- How can I clear and cleanse my space—physically or emotionally—for new growth?
- What daily rituals help me tend my inner flame?

Outdoor Practices:

- ☐ Light a candle or small fire at dawn to welcome the returning sun
- ☐ Sweep or smudge your home and outdoor spaces, symbolically clearing stagnant energy
- ☐ Offer milk, seeds, or oat cakes to the land in gratitude
- ☐ Bless water from a natural source (spring, rain, river) for cleansing and renewal

Febuary Wheel of Wellbeing

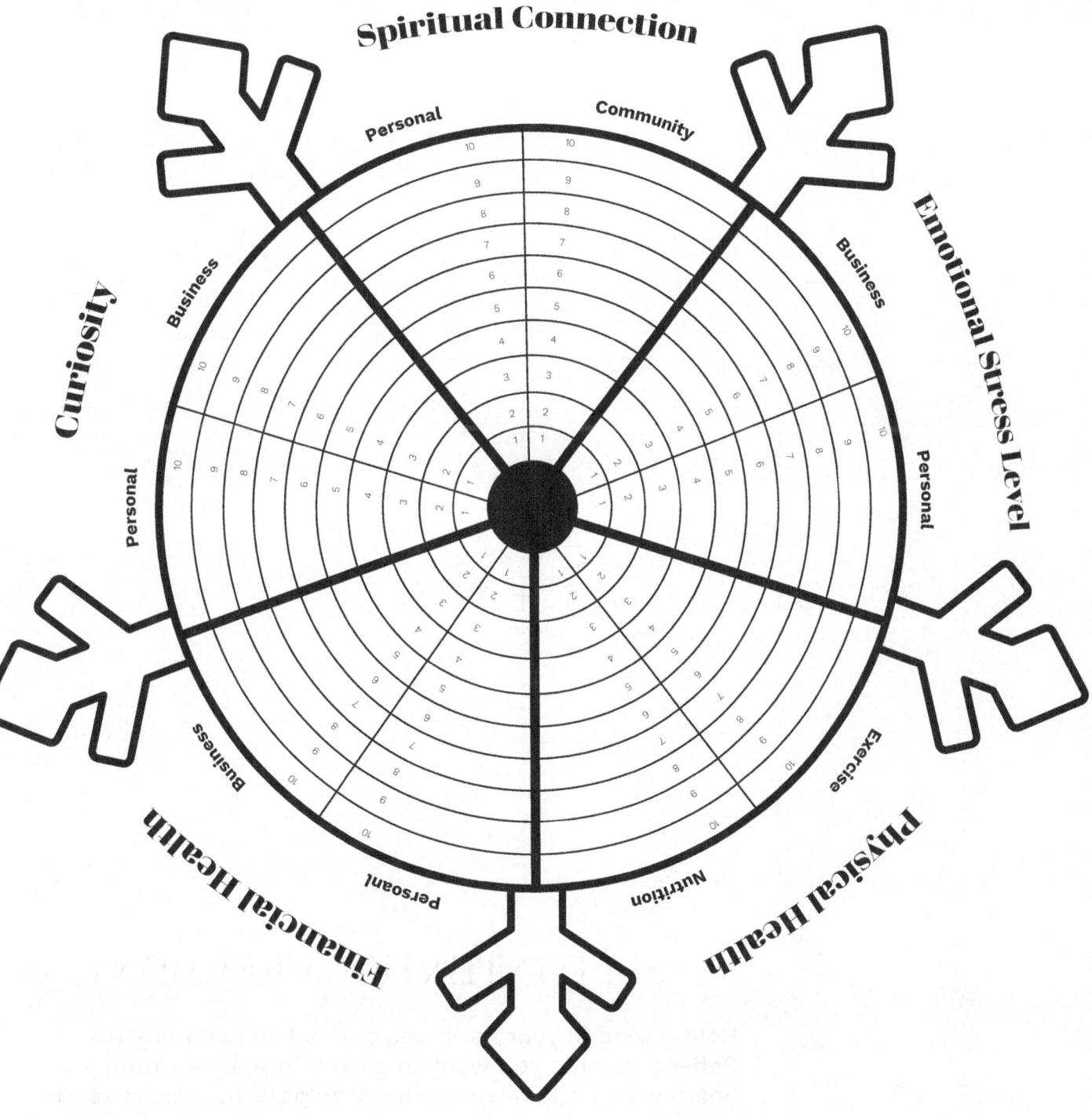

Seeds of Intention: _____
_____
_____

February

YEAR: _____

SUN	MON	TUE	WED
○	○	○	○
○	○	○	○
○	○	○	○
○	○	○	○
○	○	○	○

SEED INTENTION CEREMONY

Hold a seed in your hand and take a few deep breaths. Reflect on what you want to grow this year — within your heart, your work, or your relationships. When you're ready, plant the seed in soil or keep it somewhere special as a living reminder of your intention. Let this be a gentle promise to yourself and to the Earth that new life is on its way.

THU	FRI	SAT
○	○	○
○	○	○
○	○	○
○	○	○
○	○	○

JOURNAL PROMPT

What new energy or idea is beginning to stir in me?

February

	PRIORITIES
	1.
	2.
	3.

WEEK: _____
through _____

MONDAY

- [ ] _____
- [ ] _____
- [ ] _____
- [ ] _____
- [ ] _____
- [ ] _____

This week, look for the first subtle signs of life — a bird's song, new buds, the scent of damp earth. The world is beginning to stir. Journal your reflections: *What new energy is awakening in me? What feels ready to emerge after a time of rest?*

TUESDAY

- [ ] _____
- [ ] _____
- [ ] _____
- [ ] _____
- [ ] _____
- [ ] _____

FRIDAY

- [ ] _____
- [ ] _____
- [ ] _____
- [ ] _____
- [ ] _____
- [ ] _____

WEDNESDAY

- [ ] _____
- [ ] _____
- [ ] _____
- [ ] _____
- [ ] _____
- [ ] _____

SATURDAY

- [ ] _____
- [ ] _____
- [ ] _____
- [ ] _____
- [ ] _____
- [ ] _____

THURSDAY

- [ ] _____
- [ ] _____
- [ ] _____
- [ ] _____
- [ ] _____
- [ ] _____

SUNDAY

- [ ] _____
- [ ] _____
- [ ] _____
- [ ] _____
- [ ] _____
- [ ] _____

Color in one snowflake for each block of 17 minutes that you connect with nature per week (sit spots, mindful walks, outdoor rituals). *Aim to spend 17 minutes a day in nature.*

WEEKLY GRATITUDE

_____
_____
_____
_____
_____
_____
_____
_____

MIND: *What clarity has come to me, and how can I honor it?*

BODY: *How do I feel when I let myself fully bask in the season's warmth and abundance?*

SPIRIT: *What does it mean to shine fully, and where do I hold back?*

WEEKLY NATURE SKETCH

WEEKLY TO-DO

○ _____
○ _____
○ _____
○ _____
○ _____
○ _____
○ _____
○ _____
○ _____
○ _____
○ _____
○ _____
○ _____
○ _____
○ _____
○ _____
○ _____
○ _____

MEAL PLAN

B: _____
L: _____
D: _____

B: _____
L: _____
D: _____

B: _____
L: _____
D: _____

B: _____
L: _____
D: _____

B: _____
L: _____
D: _____

B: _____
L: _____
D: _____

B: _____
L: _____
D: _____

February

PRIORITIES
1.
2.
3.

WEEK: _____
through _____

MONDAY
- [ ] _____
- [ ] _____
- [ ] _____
- [ ] _____
- [ ] _____
- [ ] _____

Hold a small seed in your hand. Reflect on what you want to grow this year — not just goals, but qualities of being. When you're ready, plant the seed or place it somewhere visible as a symbol of your intention. Journal your reflections: *What am I planting within myself? How will I nurture it?*

TUESDAY
- [ ] _____
- [ ] _____
- [ ] _____
- [ ] _____
- [ ] _____
- [ ] _____

FRIDAY
- [ ] _____
- [ ] _____
- [ ] _____
- [ ] _____
- [ ] _____
- [ ] _____

WEDNESDAY
- [ ] _____
- [ ] _____
- [ ] _____
- [ ] _____
- [ ] _____
- [ ] _____

SATURDAY
- [ ] _____
- [ ] _____
- [ ] _____
- [ ] _____
- [ ] _____
- [ ] _____

THURSDAY
- [ ] _____
- [ ] _____
- [ ] _____
- [ ] _____
- [ ] _____
- [ ] _____

SUNDAY
- [ ] _____
- [ ] _____
- [ ] _____
- [ ] _____
- [ ] _____
- [ ] _____

Color in one snowflake for each block of 17 minutes that you connect with nature per week (sit spots, mindful walks, outdoor rituals). *Aim to spend 17 minutes a day in nature.*

WEEKLY GRATITUDE

WEEKLY NATURE SKETCH

MIND: *What clarity has come to me, and how can I honor it?*

BODY: *How do I feel when I let myself fully bask in the season's warmth and abundance?*

SPIRIT: *What does it mean to shine fully, and where do I hold back?*

WEEKLY TO-DO

MEAL PLAN

B:
L:
D:

B:
L:
D:

B:
L:
D:

B:
L:
D:

B:
L:
D:

B:
L:
D:

B:
L:
D:

February

PRIORITIES
1.
2.
3.

WEEK: _____

through _____

MONDAY
- [ ] _____
- [ ] _____
- [ ] _____
- [ ] _____
- [ ] _____
- [ ] _____

Step outside and listen. Let the sounds of the season — melting snow, wind through branches, birds returning — become your meditation. Nature is teaching you to receive before you respond. Journal your reflections: *What is life whispering to me right now? How can I listen more deeply before taking action?*

TUESDAY
- [ ] _____
- [ ] _____
- [ ] _____
- [ ] _____
- [ ] _____
- [ ] _____

FRIDAY
- [ ] _____
- [ ] _____
- [ ] _____
- [ ] _____
- [ ] _____
- [ ] _____

WEDNESDAY
- [ ] _____
- [ ] _____
- [ ] _____
- [ ] _____
- [ ] _____
- [ ] _____

SATURDAY
- [ ] _____
- [ ] _____
- [ ] _____
- [ ] _____
- [ ] _____
- [ ] _____

THURSDAY
- [ ] _____
- [ ] _____
- [ ] _____
- [ ] _____
- [ ] _____
- [ ] _____

SUNDAY
- [ ] _____
- [ ] _____
- [ ] _____
- [ ] _____
- [ ] _____
- [ ] _____

Color in one snowflake for each block of 17 minutes that you connect with nature per week (sit spots, mindful walks, outdoor rituals). *Aim to spend 17 minutes a day in nature.*

WEEKLY GRATITUDE

_____
_____
_____
_____
_____
_____
_____
_____

MIND: *What clarity has come to me, and how can I honor it?*

BODY: *How do I feel when I let myself fully bask in the season's warmth and abundance?*

SPIRIT: *What does it mean to shine fully, and where do I hold back?*

WEEKLY NATURE SKETCH

WEEKLY TO-DO

- _____
- _____
- _____
- _____
- _____
- _____
- _____
- _____
- _____
- _____
- _____
- _____
- _____
- _____
- _____
- _____
- _____
- _____
- _____

MEAL PLAN

B: _____
L: _____
D: _____

B: _____
L: _____
D: _____

B: _____
L: _____
D: _____

B: _____
L: _____
D: _____

B: _____
L: _____
D: _____

B: _____
L: _____
D: _____

B: _____
L: _____
D: _____

B: _____
L: _____
D: _____

February

	PRIORITIES
1.	
2.	
3.	

WEEK: _____

through _____

MONDAY

☐ _____
☐ _____
☐ _____
☐ _____
☐ _____
☐ _____

Notice how the light is changing — days lengthening, mornings brightening. Let the returning light remind you of your own growth. Journal your reflections: *Where is more light entering my life? How can I honor this renewal?*

TUESDAY

☐ _____
☐ _____
☐ _____
☐ _____
☐ _____
☐ _____

FRIDAY

☐ _____
☐ _____
☐ _____
☐ _____
☐ _____
☐ _____

WEDNESDAY

☐ _____
☐ _____
☐ _____
☐ _____
☐ _____
☐ _____

SATURDAY

☐ _____
☐ _____
☐ _____
☐ _____
☐ _____
☐ _____

THURSDAY

☐ _____
☐ _____
☐ _____
☐ _____
☐ _____
☐ _____

SUNDAY

☐ _____
☐ _____
☐ _____
☐ _____
☐ _____
☐ _____

Color in one snowflake for each block of 17 minutes that you connect with nature per week (sit spots, mindful walks, outdoor rituals). *Aim to spend 17 minutes a day in nature.*

WEEKLY GRATITUDE

_____
_____
_____
_____
_____
_____
_____
_____

MIND: *What clarity has come to me, and how can I honor it?*

BODY: *How do I feel when I let myself fully bask in the season's warmth and abundance?*

SPIRIT: *What does it mean to shine fully, and where do I hold back?*

WEEKLY NATURE SKETCH

WEEKLY TO-DO

- _____
- _____
- _____
- _____
- _____
- _____
- _____
- _____
- _____
- _____
- _____
- _____
- _____
- _____
- _____
- _____
- _____
- _____

MEAL PLAN

B: _____
L: _____
D: _____

B: _____
L: _____
D: _____

B: _____
L: _____
D: _____

B: _____
L: _____
D: _____

B: _____
L: _____
D: _____

B: _____
L: _____
D: _____

B: _____
L: _____
D: _____

February

PRIORITIES
1.
2.
3.

WEEK: _____

through _____

MONDAY
- ☐ _____
- ☐ _____
- ☐ _____
- ☐ _____
- ☐ _____
- ☐ _____

Find a quiet place where water gathers — a pond, puddle, or even a bowl indoors. Watch how the surface reflects light and shadow, movement and calm. Water mirrors without judgment. Journal your reflections: *What parts of myself am I ready to see with more compassion? What truth is reflected back to me in stillness?*

TUESDAY
- ☐ _____
- ☐ _____
- ☐ _____
- ☐ _____
- ☐ _____
- ☐ _____

FRIDAY
- ☐ _____
- ☐ _____
- ☐ _____
- ☐ _____
- ☐ _____
- ☐ _____

WEDNESDAY
- ☐ _____
- ☐ _____
- ☐ _____
- ☐ _____
- ☐ _____
- ☐ _____

SATURDAY
- ☐ _____
- ☐ _____
- ☐ _____
- ☐ _____
- ☐ _____
- ☐ _____

THURSDAY
- ☐ _____
- ☐ _____
- ☐ _____
- ☐ _____
- ☐ _____
- ☐ _____

SUNDAY
- ☐ _____
- ☐ _____
- ☐ _____
- ☐ _____
- ☐ _____
- ☐ _____

Color in one snowflake for each block of 17 minutes that you connect with nature per week (sit spots, mindful walks, outdoor rituals). *Aim to spend 17 minutes a day in nature.*

WEEKLY GRATITUDE

_____
_____
_____
_____
_____
_____
_____
_____

MIND: *What clarity has come to me, and how can I honor it?*

BODY: *How do I feel when I let myself fully bask in the season's warmth and abundance?*

SPIRIT: *What does it mean to shine fully, and where do I hold back?*

WEEKLY NATURE SKETCH

WEEKLY TO-DO

- _____
- _____
- _____
- _____
- _____
- _____
- _____
- _____
- _____
- _____
- _____
- _____
- _____
- _____
- _____
- _____
- _____
- _____
- _____

MEAL PLAN

B: _____
L: _____
D: _____

B: _____
L: _____
D: _____

B: _____
L: _____
D: _____

B: _____
L: _____
D: _____

B: _____
L: _____
D: _____

B: _____
L: _____
D: _____

B: _____
L: _____
D: _____

February
Sit Spot
REFLECTIONS

What is nature teaching me?

How am I growing into my true self?

What steps am I taking toward my soul's passion?

February
Sit Spot
REFLECTIONS

Journal

Journal

Journal

Journal

Journal

Journal

Early Spring
Season Mindset

One thing in nature that inspires or excites me this season is...

A positive phrase I can repeat to myself while grounded in nature is...

Someone who needs my full presence and energy this season is...

A situation that might stress me out or trip me up this season could be...

> ... and I will take a moment in nature to breathe, observe, or connect before responding as my best self.

Someone I could surprise with a nature-inspired note, gift, or moment of appreciation is...

One action I could take this season to embody excellence or bring joy to my environment is...

One bold step I could take this season that mirrors nature's courage and resilience is...

If I were a guide walking alongside myself in nature, I would encourage myself with this...

> *I would end this season feeling proud if I make sure to spend time appreciating the small, beautiful details in my life, just like noticing a flower or sunset.*

The big picture I have to keep in mind this season is that I am growing, like the cycles of nature, steadily towards...

OSTARA

MARCH 20
A Season of Balance & New Beginnings

Overview

Ostara (pronounced Oh-star-ah) celebrates the Spring Equinox—when day and night stand in perfect balance before tipping toward the light. Usually observed around March 20th–22nd, it honors fertility, growth, and rebirth. Named for the Germanic goddess Eostre, whose symbols include hares, eggs, and flowers, Ostara reminds us that life always finds a way to return. In nature, buds swell, birds build nests, and the Earth hums with vitality. This is a season of equilibrium—of honoring both our light and shadow as we plant intentions for the growing year ahead.

Nature's Invitation (Sit Spot Practice)

Find a place where new life is visible—fresh shoots, blossoms, or returning birds. Sit and notice the balance between stillness and motion, warmth and chill, day and night. Feel the energy of renewal pulsing through the land and within you. Imagine planting seeds—literal or symbolic—for what you wish to grow this season. Offer your breath or song to the wind as a blessing of gratitude.

Reflective Focus:

- Where in my life am I seeking balance or harmony?
- What seeds of intention am I ready to plant and nurture?
- How can I celebrate the joy and beauty of new beginnings?

Outdoor Practices:

- [ ] Decorate eggs or stones as symbols of fertility and creativity
- [ ] Plant seeds or tend a garden in honor of new growth
- [ ] Take a sunrise walk to greet the light of the equinox
- [ ] Create a nature mandala with flowers, twigs, and leaves to celebrate renewal

March Wheel of Wellbeing

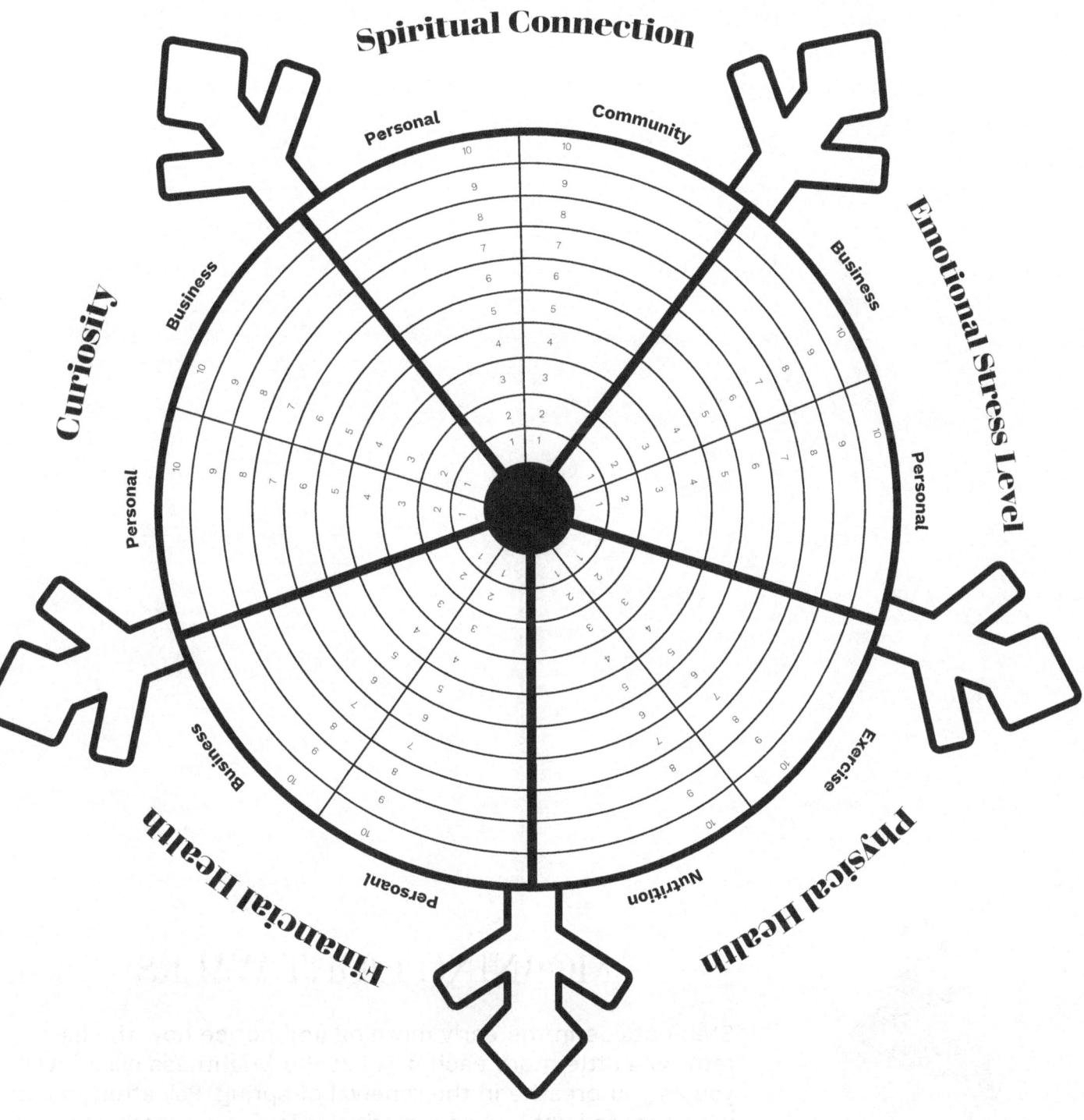

Seeds of Intention: _____
_____
_____

March

YEAR: _____

SUN	MON	TUE	WED
○	○	○	○
○	○	○	○
○	○	○	○
○	○	○	○
○	○	○	○

MORNING LIGHT WALKS

Step outside in the early morning and notice how the light returns a little more each day. Let the brightness wash over you as you breathe in the renewal of spring. Pay attention to where more light — hope, clarity, or joy — is entering your own life. Nature's rhythm reminds us that even small shifts can lead to great growth.

THU	FRI	SAT

JOURNAL PROMPT

What is ready to bloom in my life, and how can I nurture it?

March

PRIORITIES
1.
2.
3.

WEEK: _____
through _____

MONDAY
- [ ] _____
- [ ] _____
- [ ] _____
- [ ] _____
- [ ] _____
- [ ] _____

As March begins, step outside at dawn. Notice how the air feels different — softer, more alive. Take three deep breaths, imagining you are inhaling new energy. Journal your reflections: *What do I feel ready to begin? What fresh possibilities are stirring within me?*

TUESDAY
- [ ] _____
- [ ] _____
- [ ] _____
- [ ] _____
- [ ] _____
- [ ] _____

FRIDAY
- [ ] _____
- [ ] _____
- [ ] _____
- [ ] _____
- [ ] _____
- [ ] _____

WEDNESDAY
- [ ] _____
- [ ] _____
- [ ] _____
- [ ] _____
- [ ] _____
- [ ] _____

SATURDAY
- [ ] _____
- [ ] _____
- [ ] _____
- [ ] _____
- [ ] _____
- [ ] _____

THURSDAY
- [ ] _____
- [ ] _____
- [ ] _____
- [ ] _____
- [ ] _____
- [ ] _____

SUNDAY
- [ ] _____
- [ ] _____
- [ ] _____
- [ ] _____
- [ ] _____
- [ ] _____

Color in one snowflake for each block of 17 minutes that you connect with nature per week (sit spots, mindful walks, outdoor rituals). *Aim to spend 17 minutes a day in nature.*

WEEKLY GRATITUDE

_____
_____
_____
_____
_____
_____
_____
_____
_____

MIND: *What clarity has come to me, and how can I honor it?*

BODY: *How do I feel when I let myself fully bask in the season's warmth and abundance?*

SPIRIT: *What does it mean to shine fully, and where do I hold back?*

WEEKLY NATURE SKETCH

WEEKLY TO-DO

○ _____
○ _____
○ _____
○ _____
○ _____
○ _____
○ _____
○ _____
○ _____
○ _____
○ _____
○ _____
○ _____
○ _____
○ _____
○ _____
○ _____
○ _____
○ _____
○ _____

MEAL PLAN

B: _____
L: _____
D: _____

B: _____
L: _____
D: _____

B: _____
L: _____
D: _____

B: _____
L: _____
D: _____

B: _____
L: _____
D: _____

B: _____
L: _____
D: _____

B: _____
L: _____
D: _____

March

PRIORITIES
1.
2.
3.

WEEK: _____

through _____

MONDAY

☐ _____
☐ _____
☐ _____
☐ _____
☐ _____
☐ _____

> Spend a few minutes with flowing water — a stream, rain, or even water from your faucet. Watch how it moves easily around obstacles. Let this be your teacher. Journal your reflections: *Where can I allow more flow in my life? What am I trying to control that could instead move naturally?*

TUESDAY

☐ _____
☐ _____
☐ _____
☐ _____
☐ _____
☐ _____

FRIDAY

☐ _____
☐ _____
☐ _____
☐ _____
☐ _____
☐ _____

WEDNESDAY

☐ _____
☐ _____
☐ _____
☐ _____
☐ _____
☐ _____

SATURDAY

☐ _____
☐ _____
☐ _____
☐ _____
☐ _____
☐ _____

THURSDAY

☐ _____
☐ _____
☐ _____
☐ _____
☐ _____
☐ _____

SUNDAY

☐ _____
☐ _____
☐ _____
☐ _____
☐ _____
☐ _____

Color in one snowflake for each block of 17 minutes that you connect with nature per week (sit spots, mindful walks, outdoor rituals). *Aim to spend 17 minutes a day in nature.*

WEEKLY GRATITUDE

_____
_____
_____
_____
_____
_____
_____
_____

MIND: *What clarity has come to me, and how can I honor it?*

BODY: *How do I feel when I let myself fully bask in the season's warmth and abundance?*

SPIRIT: *What does it mean to shine fully, and where do I hold back?*

WEEKLY NATURE SKETCH

WEEKLY TO-DO

- _____
- _____
- _____
- _____
- _____
- _____
- _____
- _____
- _____
- _____
- _____
- _____
- _____
- _____
- _____
- _____
- _____
- _____

MEAL PLAN

B: _____
L: _____
D: _____

B: _____
L: _____
D: _____

B: _____
L: _____
D: _____

B: _____
L: _____
D: _____

B: _____
L: _____
D: _____

B: _____
L: _____
D: _____

B: _____
L: _____
D: _____

March

	PRIORITIES
1.	
2.	
3.	

WEEK: _____

through _____

MONDAY

☐ _____
☐ _____
☐ _____
☐ _____
☐ _____
☐ _____

As the Spring Equinox nears, gather something green — a sprig of new growth, a leaf, a blade of grass. Place it in your journal as a symbol of renewal. Journal your reflections: What is ready to bloom in me? How can I make space for new life to grow?

TUESDAY

☐ _____
☐ _____
☐ _____
☐ _____
☐ _____
☐ _____

FRIDAY

☐ _____
☐ _____
☐ _____
☐ _____
☐ _____
☐ _____

WEDNESDAY

☐ _____
☐ _____
☐ _____
☐ _____
☐ _____
☐ _____

SATURDAY

☐ _____
☐ _____
☐ _____
☐ _____
☐ _____
☐ _____

THURSDAY

☐ _____
☐ _____
☐ _____
☐ _____
☐ _____
☐ _____

SUNDAY

☐ _____
☐ _____
☐ _____
☐ _____
☐ _____
☐ _____

Color in one snowflake for each block of 17 minutes that you connect with nature per week (sit spots, mindful walks, outdoor rituals). *Aim to spend 17 minutes a day in nature.*

WEEKLY GRATITUDE

_____
_____
_____
_____
_____
_____
_____
_____

MIND: *What clarity has come to me, and how can I honor it?*

BODY: *How do I feel when I let myself fully bask in the season's warmth and abundance?*

SPIRIT: *What does it mean to shine fully, and where do I hold back?*

WEEKLY NATURE SKETCH

WEEKLY TO-DO

- _____
- _____
- _____
- _____
- _____
- _____
- _____
- _____
- _____
- _____
- _____
- _____
- _____
- _____
- _____
- _____
- _____
- _____

MEAL PLAN

B: _____
L: _____
D: _____

B: _____
L: _____
D: _____

B: _____
L: _____
D: _____

B: _____
L: _____
D: _____

B: _____
L: _____
D: _____

B: _____
L: _____
D: _____

B: _____
L: _____
D: _____

March

PRIORITIES	
1.	
2.	
3.	

WEEK: _____

through _____

MONDAY

- [ ] _____
- [ ] _____
- [ ] _____
- [ ] _____
- [ ] _____
- [ ] _____

With the balance of day and night upon us, reflect on your own balance. What have you nurtured this season? What needs more care? Step outside and feel the warmth on your face — a promise of what's to come. Journal your reflections: *What harmony am I cultivating between rest and action? How can I carry this balance forward into spring?*

TUESDAY

- [ ] _____
- [ ] _____
- [ ] _____
- [ ] _____
- [ ] _____
- [ ] _____

FRIDAY

- [ ] _____
- [ ] _____
- [ ] _____
- [ ] _____
- [ ] _____
- [ ] _____

WEDNESDAY

- [ ] _____
- [ ] _____
- [ ] _____
- [ ] _____
- [ ] _____
- [ ] _____

SATURDAY

- [ ] _____
- [ ] _____
- [ ] _____
- [ ] _____
- [ ] _____
- [ ] _____

THURSDAY

- [ ] _____
- [ ] _____
- [ ] _____
- [ ] _____
- [ ] _____
- [ ] _____

SUNDAY

- [ ] _____
- [ ] _____
- [ ] _____
- [ ] _____
- [ ] _____
- [ ] _____

Color in one snowflake for each block of 17 minutes that you connect with nature per week (sit spots, mindful walks, outdoor rituals). *Aim to spend 17 minutes a day in nature.*

WEEKLY GRATITUDE

_____
_____
_____
_____
_____
_____
_____
_____

MIND: *What clarity has come to me, and how can I honor it?*

BODY: *How do I feel when I let myself fully bask in the season's warmth and abundance?*

SPIRIT: *What does it mean to shine fully, and where do I hold back?*

WEEKLY NATURE SKETCH

WEEKLY TO-DO

- _____
- _____
- _____
- _____
- _____
- _____
- _____
- _____
- _____
- _____
- _____
- _____
- _____
- _____
- _____
- _____
- _____

MEAL PLAN

B: _____
L: _____
D: _____

B: _____
L: _____
D: _____

B: _____
L: _____
D: _____

B: _____
L: _____
D: _____

B: _____
L: _____
D: _____

B: _____
L: _____
D: _____

B: _____
L: _____
D: _____

March

PRIORITIES	
1.	
2.	
3.	

WEEK: _____

through _____

MONDAY

- [ ] _____
- [ ] _____
- [ ] _____
- [ ] _____
- [ ] _____
- [ ] _____

Notice the quality of sunlight today — where it lands, how it shifts, the warmth or coolness it carries. Light changes everything, yet never asks for attention. Journal your reflections: *Where am I being invited to shine more freely? What does "light" mean in my life right now — clarity, joy, forgiveness, or something else?*

TUESDAY

- [ ] _____
- [ ] _____
- [ ] _____
- [ ] _____
- [ ] _____
- [ ] _____

FRIDAY

- [ ] _____
- [ ] _____
- [ ] _____
- [ ] _____
- [ ] _____
- [ ] _____

WEDNESDAY

- [ ] _____
- [ ] _____
- [ ] _____
- [ ] _____
- [ ] _____
- [ ] _____

SATURDAY

- [ ] _____
- [ ] _____
- [ ] _____
- [ ] _____
- [ ] _____
- [ ] _____

THURSDAY

- [ ] _____
- [ ] _____
- [ ] _____
- [ ] _____
- [ ] _____
- [ ] _____

SUNDAY

- [ ] _____
- [ ] _____
- [ ] _____
- [ ] _____
- [ ] _____
- [ ] _____

Color in one snowflake for each block of 17 minutes that you connect with nature per week (sit spots, mindful walks, outdoor rituals). *Aim to spend 17 minutes a day in nature.*

WEEKLY GRATITUDE

_____
_____
_____
_____
_____
_____
_____
_____
_____

MIND: *What clarity has come to me, and how can I honor it?*

BODY: *How do I feel when I let myself fully bask in the season's warmth and abundance?*

SPIRIT: *What does it mean to shine fully, and where do I hold back?*

WEEKLY NATURE SKETCH

WEEKLY TO-DO

- _____
- _____
- _____
- _____
- _____
- _____
- _____
- _____
- _____
- _____
- _____
- _____
- _____
- _____
- _____
- _____
- _____
- _____

MEAL PLAN

B: _____
L: _____
D: _____

B: _____
L: _____
D: _____

B: _____
L: _____
D: _____

B: _____
L: _____
D: _____

B: _____
L: _____
D: _____

B: _____
L: _____
D: _____

B: _____
L: _____
D: _____

March
Sit Spot
REFLECTIONS

What is nature teaching me?

How am I growing into my true self?

What steps am I taking toward my soul's passion?

March
Sit Spot
REFLECTIONS

Journal

Journal

Journal

Journal

Journal

Seasonal Scorecard

Rate yourself (1-5) on these nature-connected high-performance habits.
The goal is mindfulness, not perfection.

① ② ③ ④ ⑤ **CLARITY**

I aligned with my inner wisdom and grounded my intentions by spending time in nature's stillness this season.

① ② ③ ④ ⑤ **PRODUCTIVITY**

I focused on what mattered most, moving with the natural flow of the day and allowing space for calm, presence, and nature's guidance.

① ② ③ ④ ⑤ **ENERGY**

I honored my mental, physical, and emotional energy by following natural rhythms — embracing light, rest, movement, and time outdoors.

① ② ③ ④ ⑤ **CONNECTION**

I nurtured relationships with others and with the living world around me — pausing to listen, notice, and be fully present in nature's embrace.

① ② ③ ④ ⑤ **PURPOSE**

I showed up as my truest self, drawing inspiration from the cycles, seasons, and wisdom of the Earth.

① ② ③ ④ ⑤ **COURAGE**

I expressed my authentic self with honesty and resilience, like nature itself — unafraid to stand in my truth and beauty.

Winter & Early Spring
Season Reflection

Think back on the last 3 months and answer...

A moment I truly appreciated or felt gratitude in nature last season was...

A situation or task I handled well, with calmness and balance, was...

Something I realized or learned from observing nature or being in a natural setting was...

I could have made last season even better if I had paused to notice...

Something that could have helped me feel more connected to others or to the natural world last season would have been...

If I were reflecting with myself at a sit spot in nature, I would tell myself this about my season...

Emotions Wheel

The Emotions Wheel is a powerful tool for deepening emotional awareness, especially during times of reflection, healing, or nature-connected journaling. To use it, begin by identifying a core feeling you're experiencing—one of the central emotions in the inner circle such as Sad, Angry, Fearful, Happy, Disgusted, or Surprised. Then, move outward through the layers to explore the nuances of that emotion. For example, if you feel Sad, you might notice it's not just sadness—it could be Lonely, and within that, you may recognize a deeper feeling of Abandonment. By tracing your experience outward, you gain clarity about what you're really feeling, which opens space for compassion, processing, and integration. This practice can be especially helpful after a sit spot, seasonal ritual, or during inner reflection. Use the wheel as a nonjudgmental guide—there are no wrong answers, only deeper truths waiting to be named and honored.

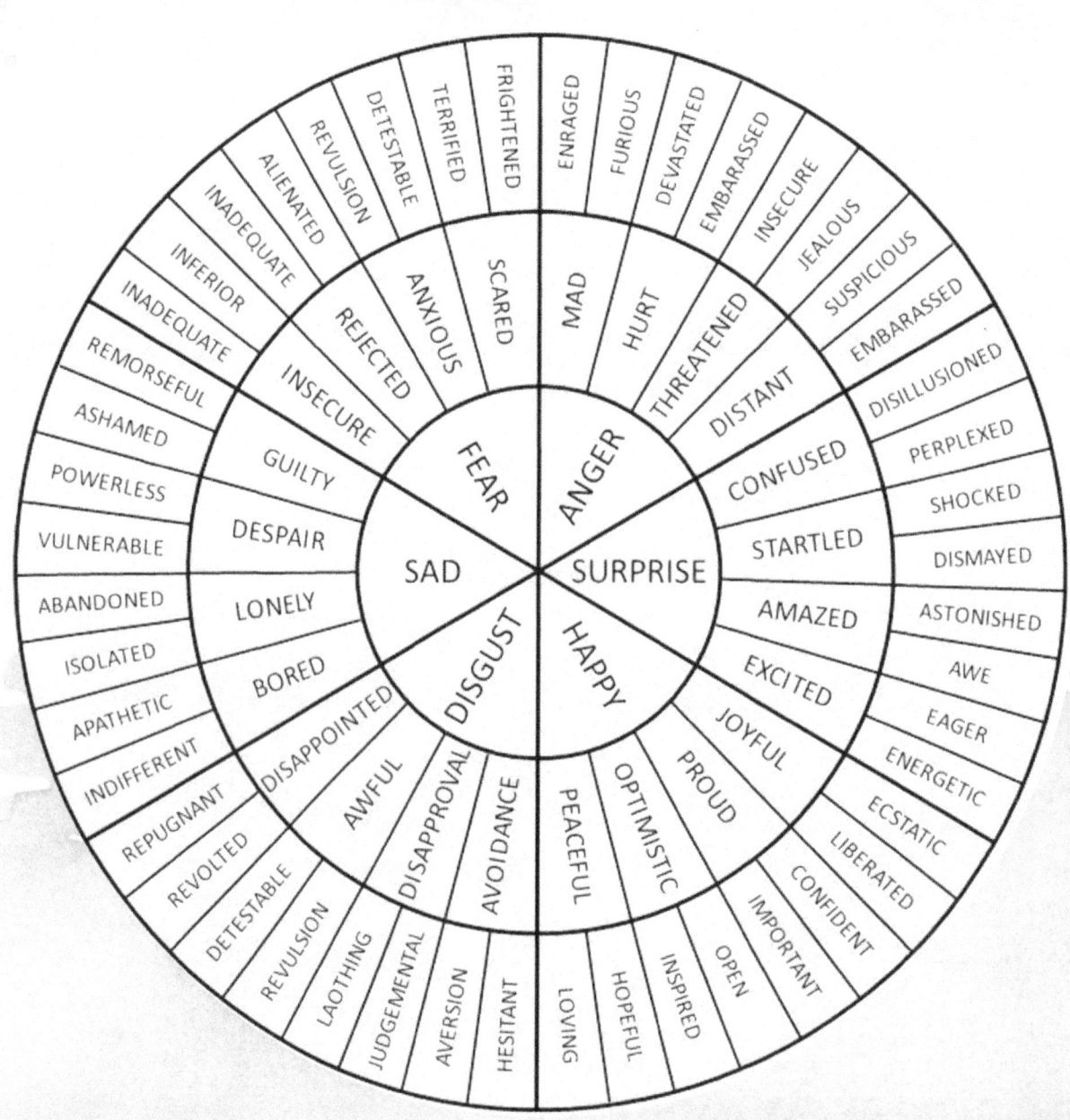

Nature Pyramid

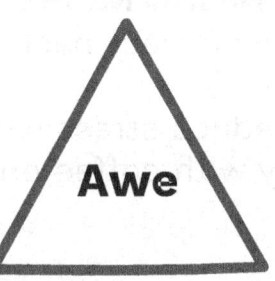

- **Awe**
- **Yearly Nature:** Go Somewhere New
- **Monthly Trips:** Support Your State Parks
- **Weekly Exploration:** Visit a Local Nature Area and Explore
- **Apple-a-Day Nature:** Daily Trips to Your Own Nearby Nature

Discover the Power of Nature with Inner-NATURALIST

Nature has the power to restore, rejuvenate, and inspire. By incorporating nature into your daily routine, you can transform your well-being. Follow the Nature Pyramid to bring more wholeness and joy into your life:

- **Apple-a-Day Nature: Daily Nearby Nature**
    - Spend 5-10 minutes daily in your backyard, local park, or a tree-lined street.
    - Boost your mood and reduce stress with just 5 minutes outdoors.
    - Example: Start your day with coffee on your porch, listening to birds and feeling the breeze.

- **Weekly Exploration: Visit a Local Nature Area**
    - Explore local parks, trails, or nature reserves weekly.
    - Disconnect from daily life and reconnect with yourself.
    - Example: Hike at your nearest state park or take a scenic bike ride on Sundays.

- **Monthly Trips: Support Your National & State Parks**
    - Commit to a monthly trip to a state or national park.
    - Experience different environments for reflection and renewal.
    - Example: Plan a weekend getaway to a nearby state park for hiking, camping, and relaxation.

- **Yearly Nature: Experience Awe in New Places**
    - Take a yearly trip to an awe-inspiring destination.
    - Reflect, grow, and transform in the wonders of nature.
    - Example: Join Inner-NATURALIST for an awe inspiring retreat

Why Nature Connected Coaching?

- Use nature as a tool for personal growth and healing.
- Overcome challenges, reduce stress, and bring more joy into your life.
- Learn to harness the cycles and seasons of nature.

Join Us on the Journey to Wholeness and Joy!

Explore our website: www.inner-naturalist.com

Email us: yourinnernaturalist@gmail.com

Journal

Journal

Journal

Journal

Journal

Journal

Journal

Journal

Journal

Journal

Journal

ABOUT THE AUTHOR

Hi, I'm Lari Jo—a Nature Connected Transformational Coach, a lifelong lover of the outdoors, and someone who found her way back to wholeness through the wisdom of the natural world.

My path here hasn't been straight. Like so many of us, I've walked through seasons of grief, stress, burnout, and deep change. I've been a daughter caring for aging parents, a mom navigating the shifting needs of a blended family, and a woman rediscovering herself after divorce. During those times, nature was not just a place to escape—it became my mirror, my teacher, and my sanctuary.

What I've come to believe—and now teach—is this: **We are not separate from nature. We *are* nature.**

Just like trees drop their leaves, rivers shift course, or tides rise and fall, we too move through cycles of becoming, resting, grieving, and renewing. When we reconnect with those rhythms, something inside us heals. We feel more grounded, more resilient, and more ourselves.

That's the heart of my work through **Inner-NATURALIST**: helping people reconnect to their own nature, using the outer world as a gentle guide. Whether it's a 17-minute pause under a tree, a seasonal journaling practice, or a once-in-a-lifetime retreat into the wild, every step into nature brings us closer to our truth.

To support that journey, I offer tools like:
- Sit spots and sensory awareness
- Seasonal reflection practices
- Guided nature walks and storytelling
- Neurographic drawing to unlock subconscious insight

Each tool is grounded in the cycle of the seasons—because when we stop pushing ourselves to bloom during winter, and instead learn to honor each season for what it brings, we begin to live more peacefully, more powerfully, and more in tune with our natural selves.

So wherever you are right now—feeling stuck, seeking something more, or simply curious—know this: You are welcome here.

Let's walk this path together and rediscover what it means to live in harmony with nature's wisdom—and your own. Let's grow together.

Happy Nature Connecting!

—Lari Jo

Made in the USA
Coppell, TX
16 January 2026

67486890R00059